FINGERPICKING
Wedding

2ND EDITION

ISBN 978-0-634-09208-4

HAL•LEONARD® CORPORATION
7777 W. BLUEMOUND RD. P.O. BOX 13819 MILWAUKEE, WI 53213

Visit Hal Leonard Online at
www.halleonard.com

CONTENTS

INTRODUCTION TO FINGERSTYLE GUITAR

Fingerstyle (a.k.a. fingerpicking) is a guitar technique that means you literally pick the strings with your right-hand fingers and thumb. This contrasts with the conventional technique of strumming and playing single notes with a pick (a.k.a. flatpicking). For fingerpicking, you can use any type of guitar: acoustic steel-string, nylon-string classical, or electric.

THE RIGHT HAND

The most common right-hand position is shown here.

Use a high wrist; arch your palm as if you were holding a ping-pong ball. Keep the thumb outside and away from the fingers, and let the fingers do the work rather than lifting your whole hand.

The thumb generally plucks the bottom strings with downstrokes on the left side of the thumb and thumbnail. The other fingers pluck the higher strings using upstrokes with the fleshy tip of the fingers and fingernails. The thumb and fingers should pluck one string per stroke and not brush over several strings.

Another picking option you may choose to use is called hybrid picking (a.k.a. plectrum-style fingerpicking). Here, the pick is usually held between the thumb and first finger, and the three remaining fingers are assigned to pluck the higher strings.

THE LEFT HAND

The left-hand fingers are numbered 1 through 4.

Be sure to keep your fingers arched, with each joint bent; if they flatten out across the strings, they will deaden the sound when you fingerpick. As a general rule, let the strings ring as long as possible when playing fingerstyle.

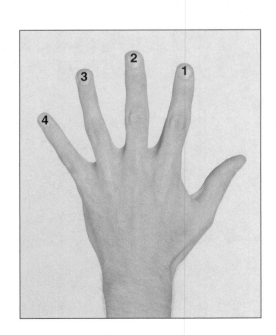

Endless Love

Words and Music by Lionel Richie

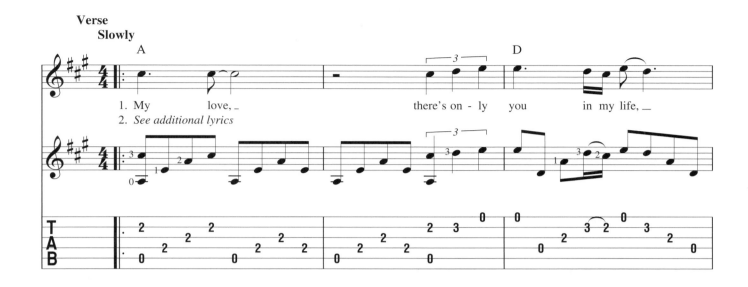

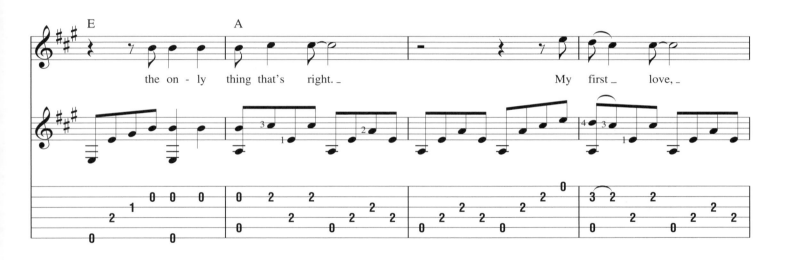

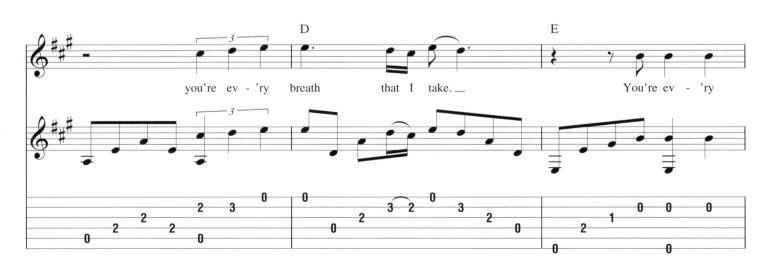

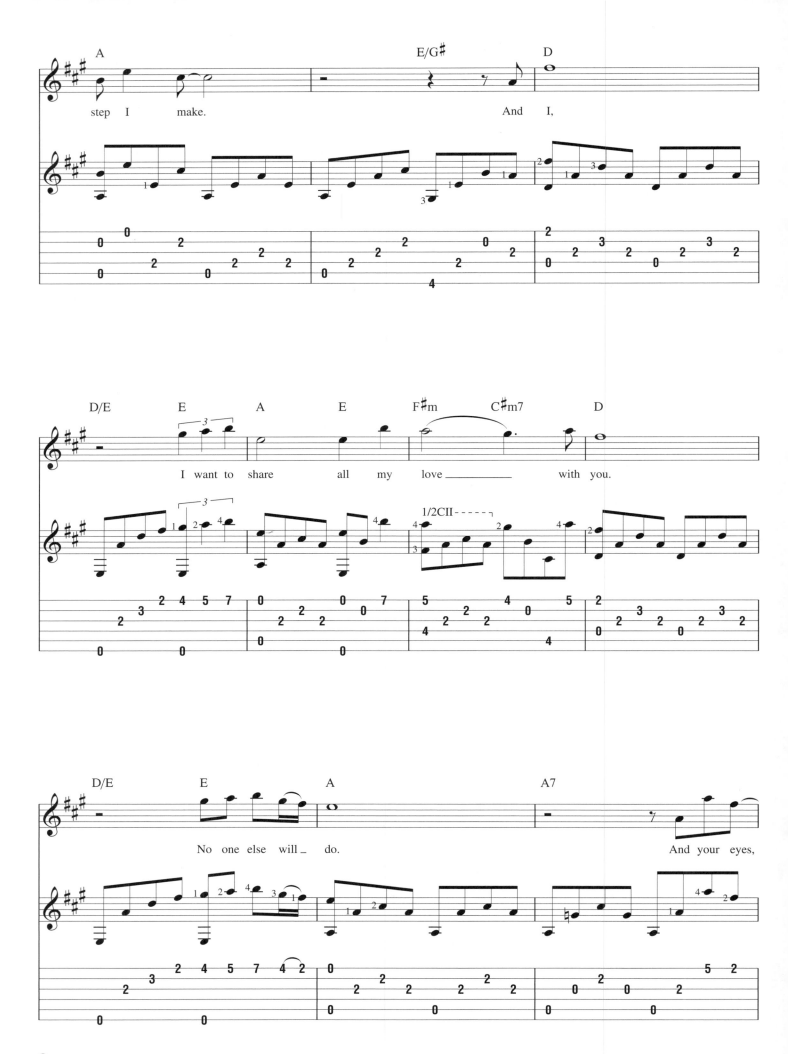

Additional Lyrics

2. Two hearts, two hearts that beat as one.
   Our lives have just begun.
   Forever I'll hold you close in my arms.
   I can't resist your charm.
   And love, I'll be a fool for you, I'm sure.
   You know I don't mind.
   'Cause you, you mean the world to me.
   Oh yes, I've found in you my endless love.

Don't Know Much

Words and Music by Barry Mann, Cynthia Weil and Tom Snow

Drop D tuning:
(low to high) D-A-D-G-B-E

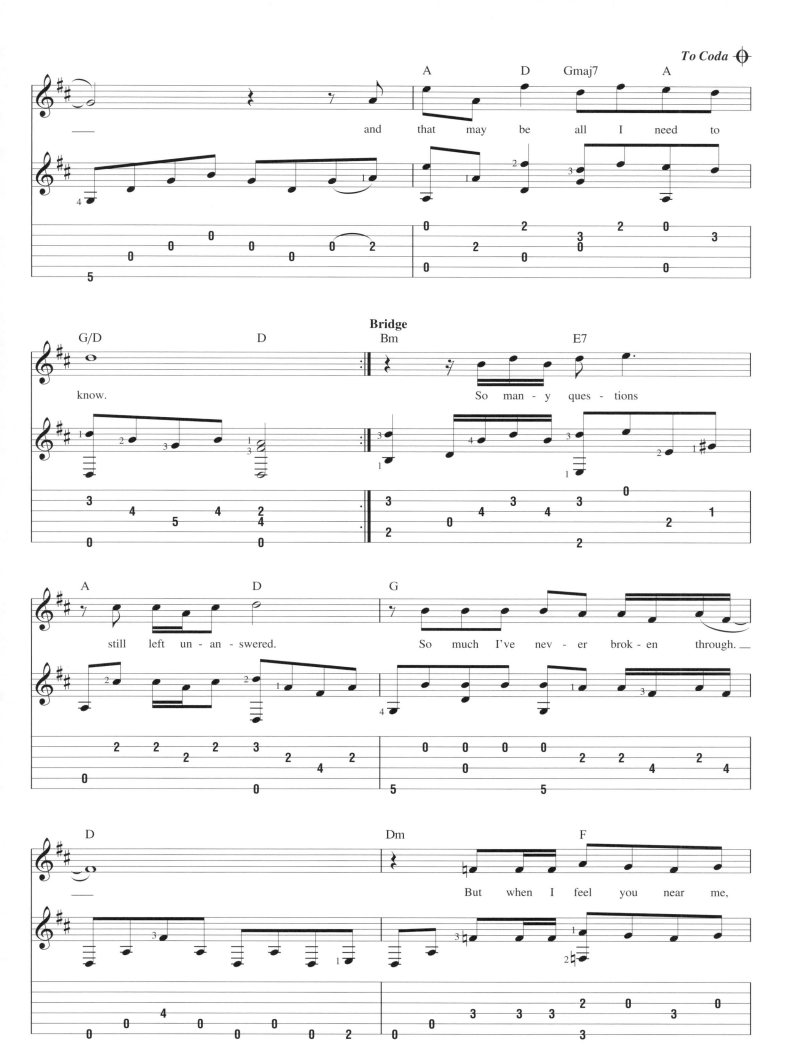

some - times I see so clear - ly   the on - ly truth I've ev - ②

known   is   me   and   you.

D.C. al Coda

Coda

know.

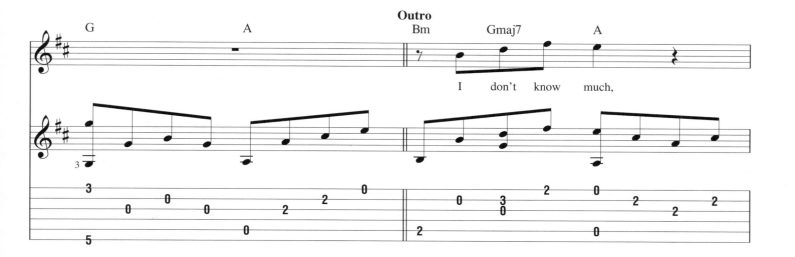

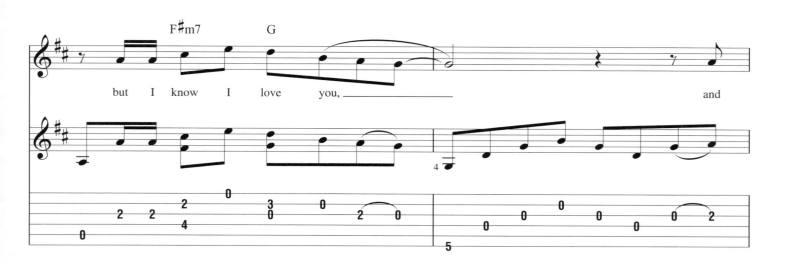

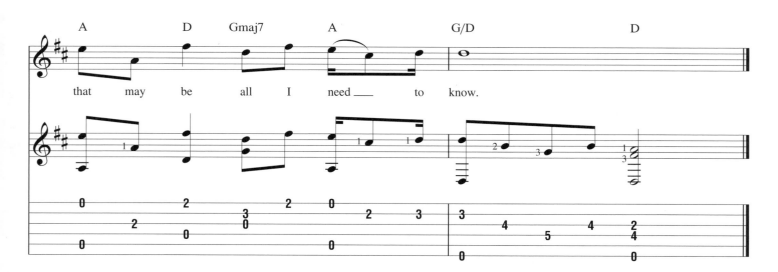

Additional Lyrics

2. Look at these eyes, they never seen what matters.
   Look at these dreams so beaten and so battered.
   I don't much, but I know I love you,
   And that may be all I need to know.

3. Look at this man so blessed with inspiration.
   Look at this soul still searching for salvation.
   I don't much, but I know I love you,
   And that may be all I need to know.

(Everything I Do) I Do It For You

from the Motion Picture ROBIN HOOD: PRINCE OF THIEVES

Words and Music by Bryan Adams, R.J. Lange and Michael Kamen

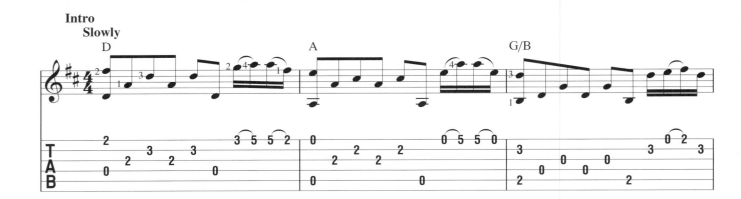

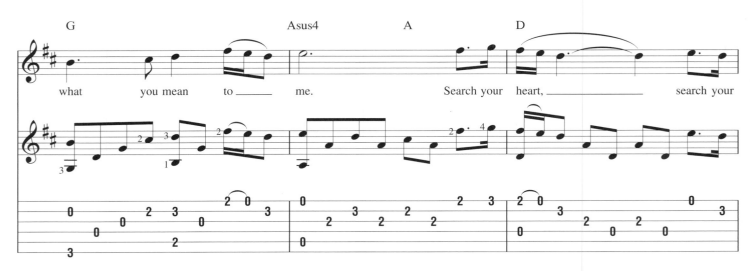

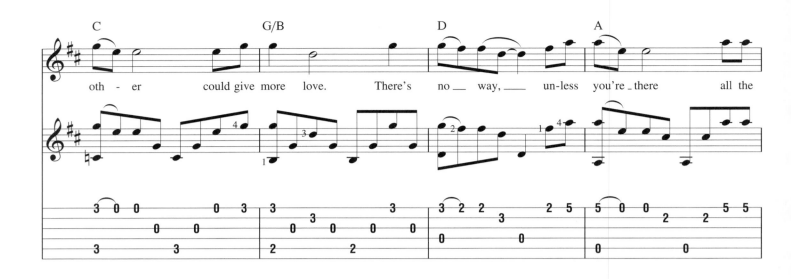

oth - er could give more love. There's no __ way, __ un-less you're _ there all the

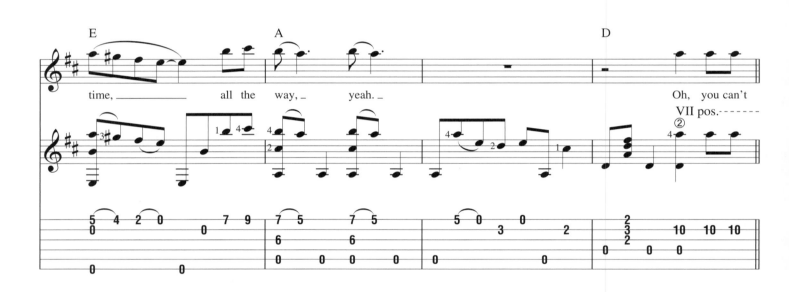

time, _____ all the way, _ yeah. _ Oh, you can't

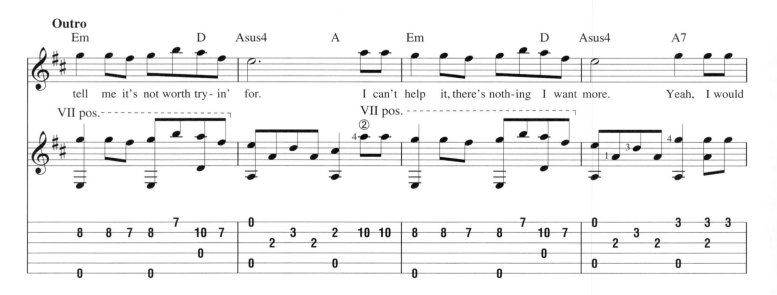

Outro

tell me it's not worth try- in' for. I can't help it, there's noth-ing I want more. Yeah, I would

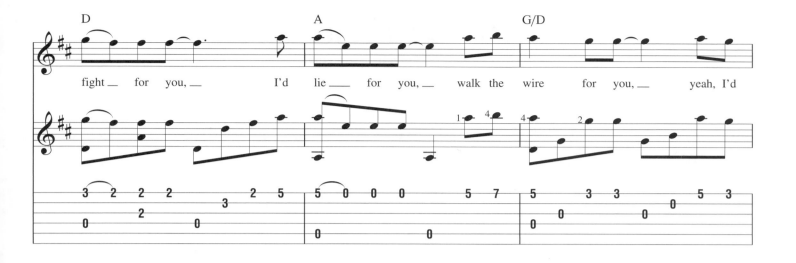

fight __ for you, __ I'd lie __ for you, __ walk the wire for you, __ yeah, I'd

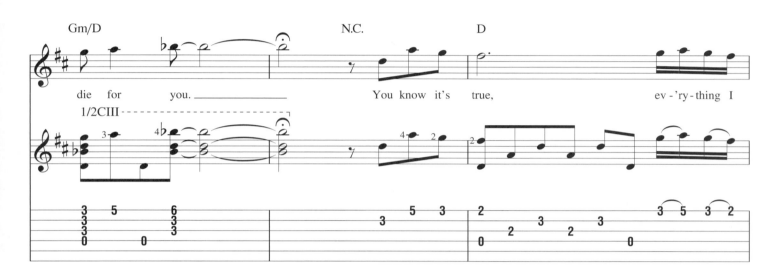

die for you. _____ You know it's true, ev-'ry-thing I

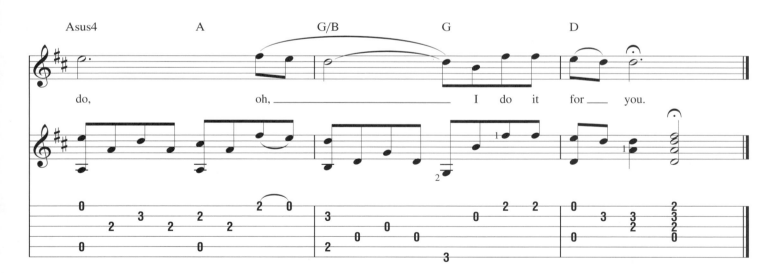

do, oh, _____ I do it for __ you.

Additional Lyrics

2. Look into your heart, you will find,
There's nothing there to hide.
Take me as I am, take my life,
I would give it all, I would sacrifice.
Don't tell me it's not worth fighting for.
I can't help it, there's nothing I want more.
You know it's true, ev'rything I do,
I do it for you.

Grow Old with Me

Words and Music by John Lennon

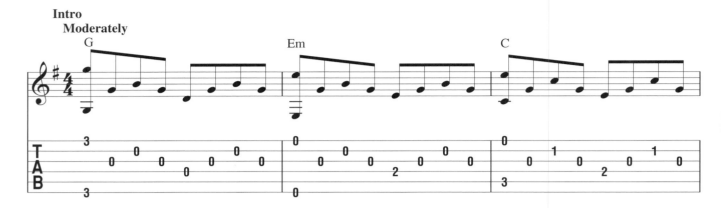

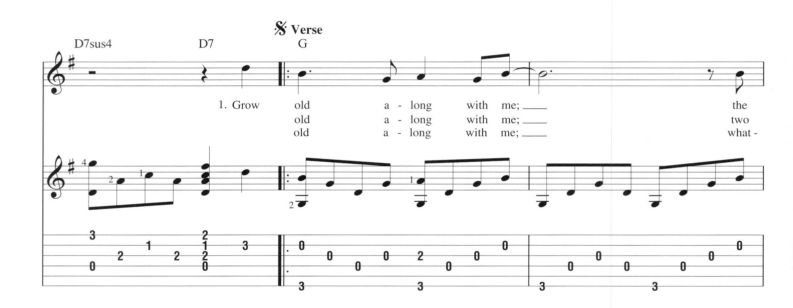

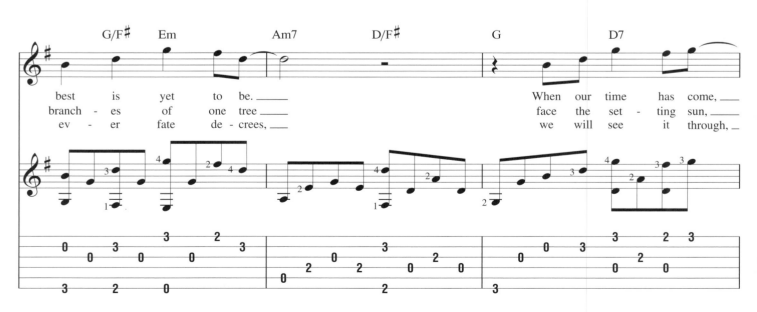

Hallelujah

Words and Music by Leonard Cohen

Verse
Moderately

1. I've heard there was a se - cret chord _ that Da - vid played _ and it
2., 3., 4., 5. *See additional lyrics*

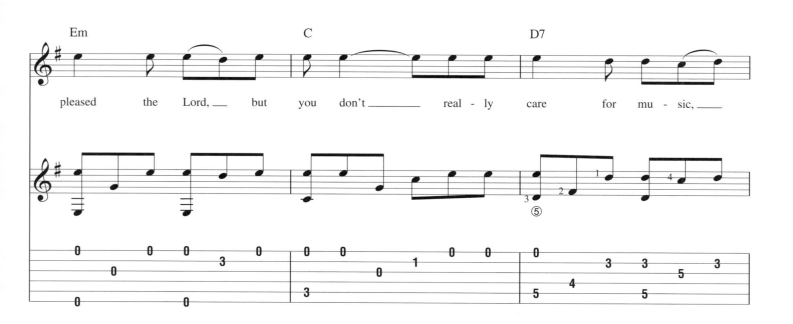

pleased the Lord, _ but you don't _____ real - ly care for mu - sic, _____

do you? _____ It goes like this: the

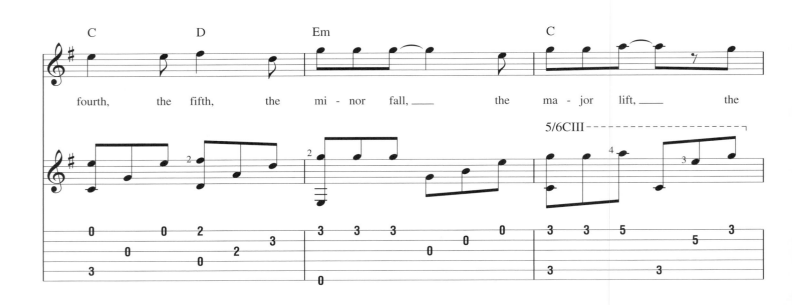

fourth, the fifth, the mi - nor fall, ___ the ma - jor lift, ___ the

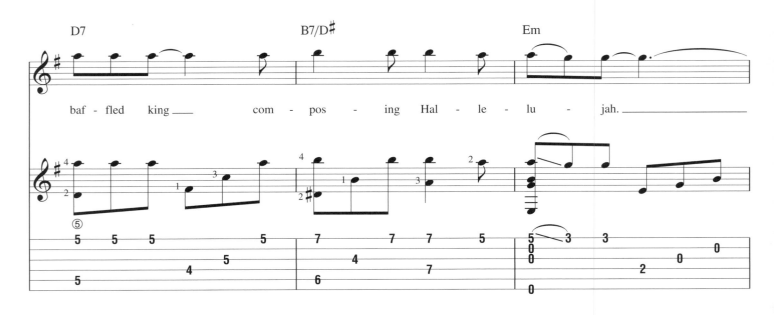

baf - fled king ___ com - pos - ing Hal - le - lu - jah. _____

Chorus

Hal - le - lu - jah, _____ Hal - le -

lu - jah, _____ Hal - le - lu - jah, _____ Hal - le -

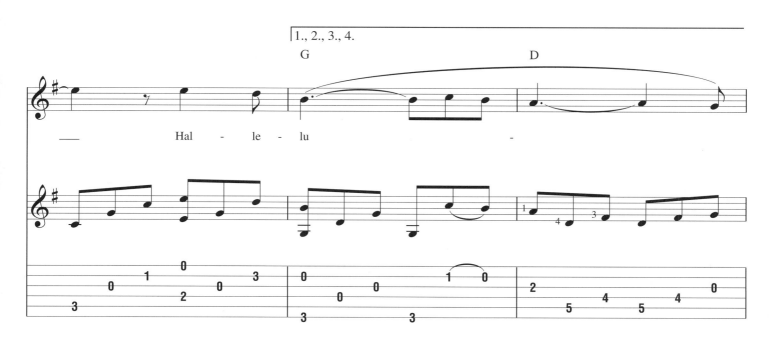

Hal - le - lu -

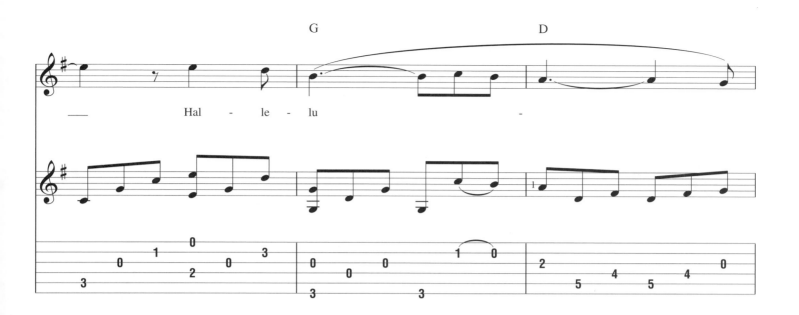

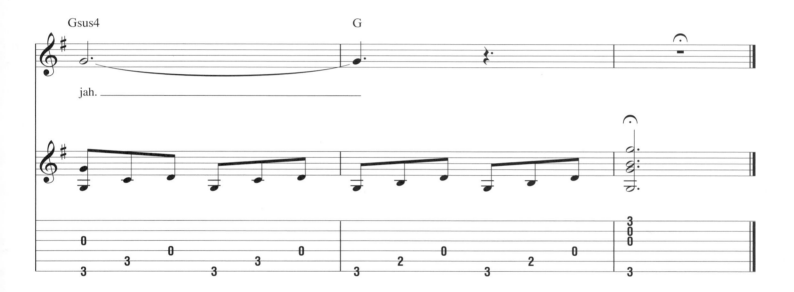

Additional Lyrics

2. Your faith was strong, but you needed proof.
   You saw her bathing on the roof.
   Her beauty and the moonlight overthrew you.
   She tied you to a kitchen chair,
   She broke your throne, she cut your hair,
   And from your lips she drew the Hallelujah.

3. Maybe I have been here before.
   I know this room, I've walked this floor.
   I used to live alone before I knew you.
   I've seen your flag on the marble arch.
   Love is not a vict'ry march,
   It's a cold and it's a broken Hallelujah.

4. There was a time you let me know
   What's really going on below,
   But now you never show it to me, do you?
   And remember when I moved in you
   The holy dove was movin' too,
   And every breath we drew was Hallelujah.

5. Maybe there's a God above,
   And all I ever learned from love
   Was how to shoot at someone who outdrew you.
   It's not a cry you can hear at night,
   It's not somebody who's seen the light,
   It's a cold and it's a broken Hallelujah.

I Will Be Here

Words and Music by Steven Curtis Chapman

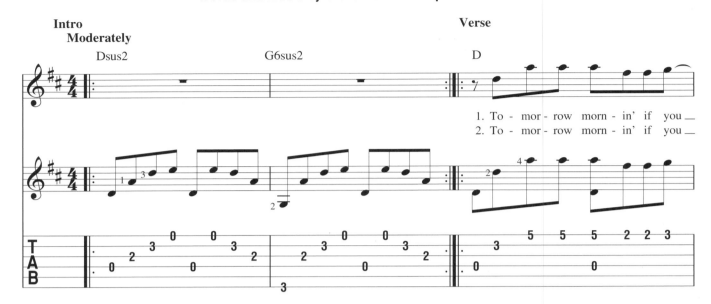

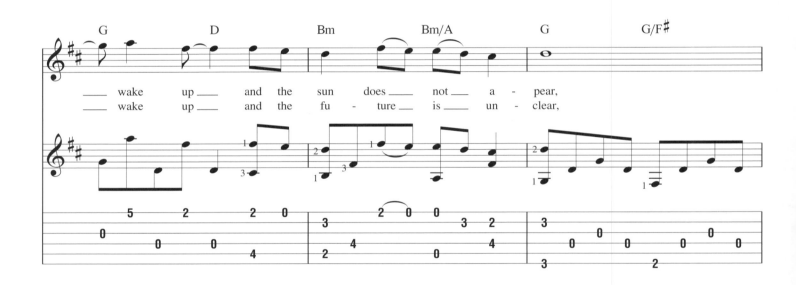

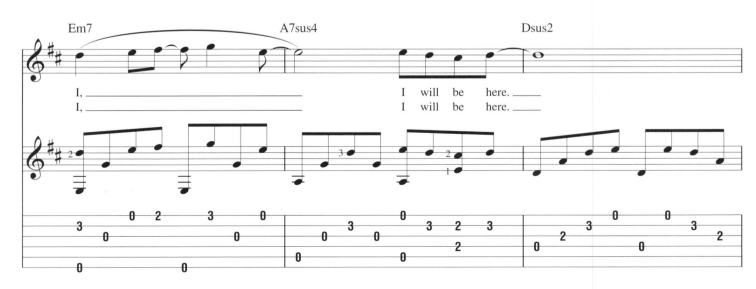

26

me. I will be here.

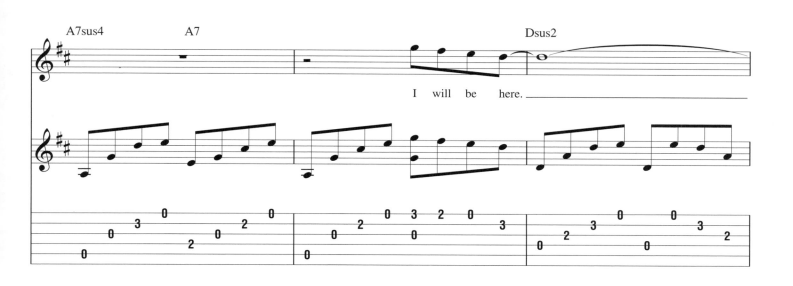

I will be here.

In My Life

Words and Music by John Lennon and Paul McCartney

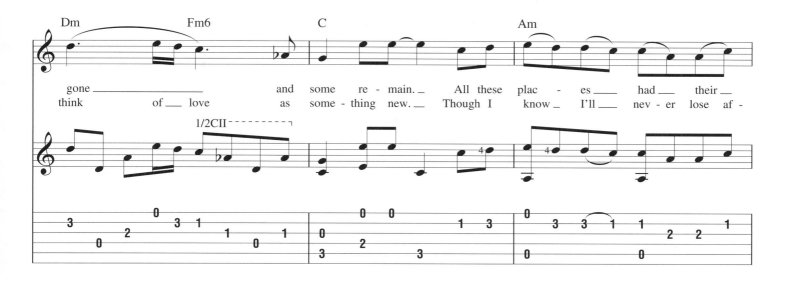

gone _____ and some re - main. ___ All these plac - es ___ had ___ their ___
think of ___ love as some - thing new. ___ Though I know ___ I'll ___ nev - er lose af -

mo - ments with lov - ers and friends ___ I still can re - call. ___ Some are
fec - tion for peo - ple and things ___ that went be - fore. ___ I

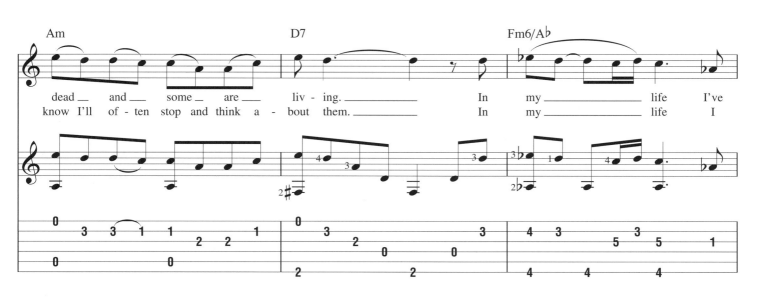

dead ___ and ___ some ___ are ___ liv - ing. ___ In my ___ life I've
know I'll of - ten stop and think a - bout them. ___ In my ___ life I

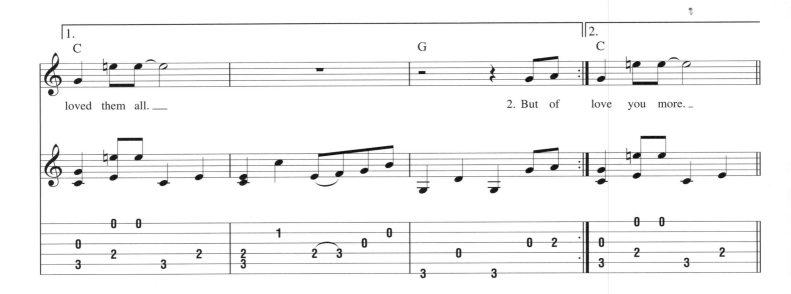

loved them all. ___

2. But of love you more. __

Outro

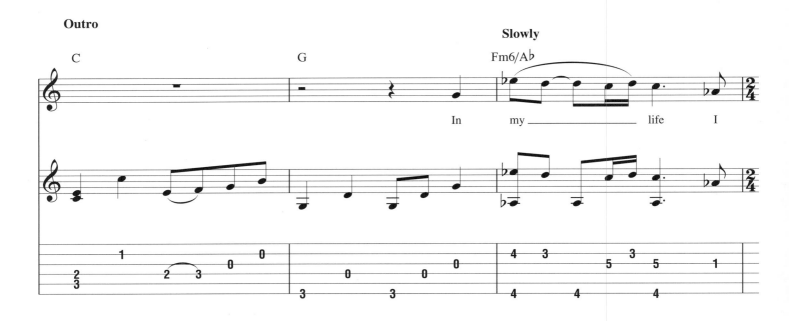

Slowly

Fm6/A♭

In my _____ life I

A tempo

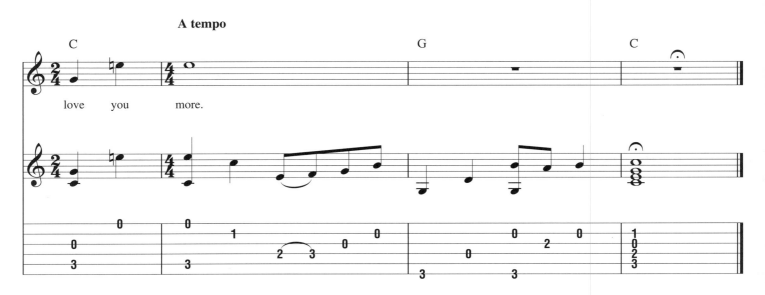

love you more.

Longer

Words and Music by Dan Fogelberg

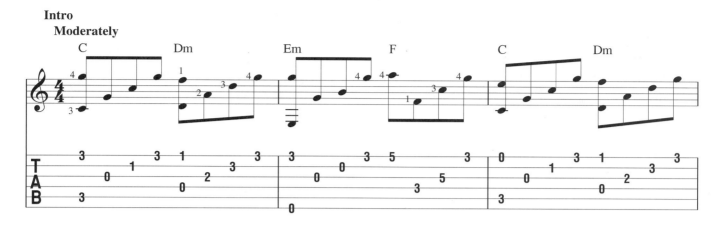

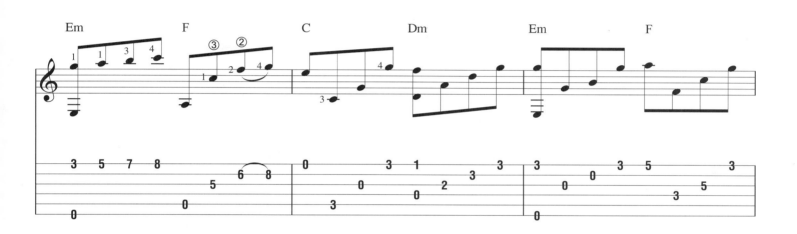

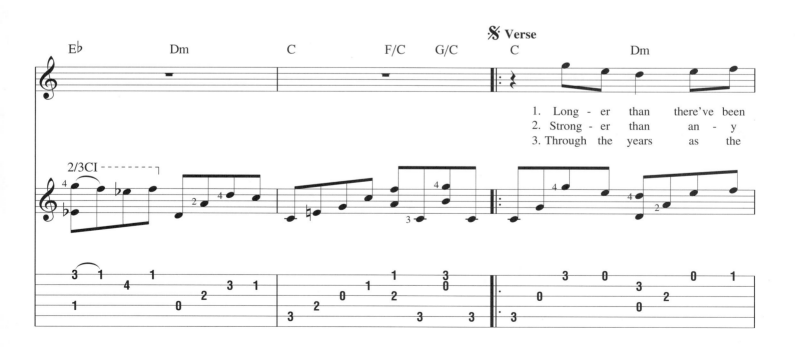

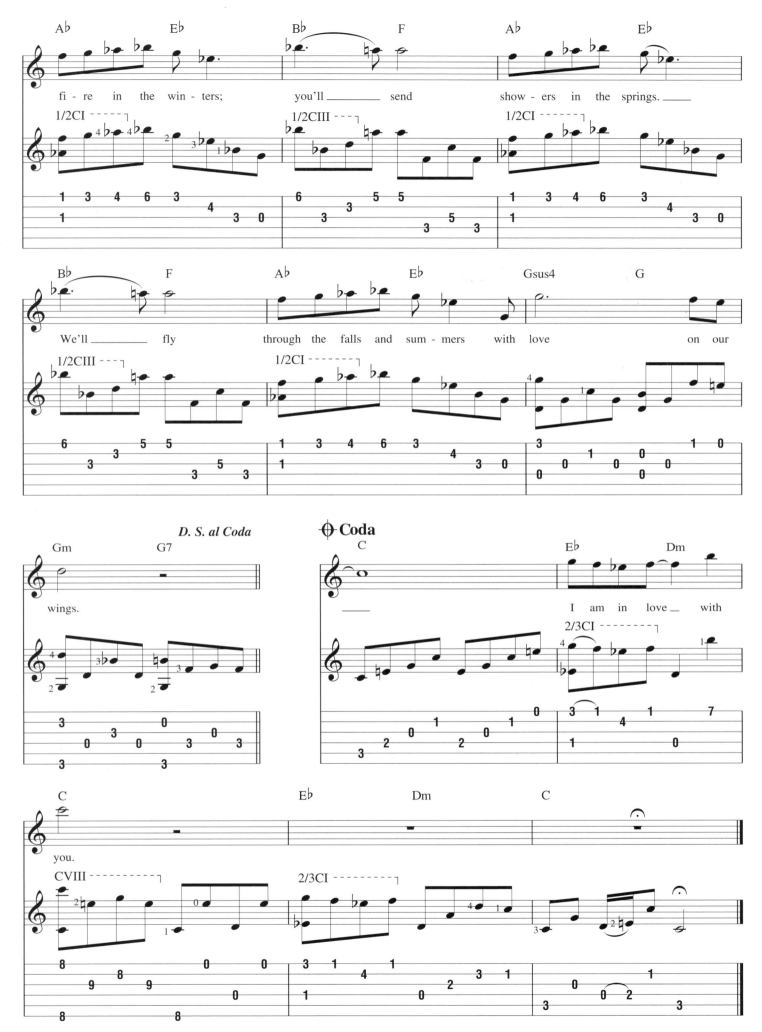

The Lord's Prayer

By Albert H. Malotte

Intro
Slowly, with expression

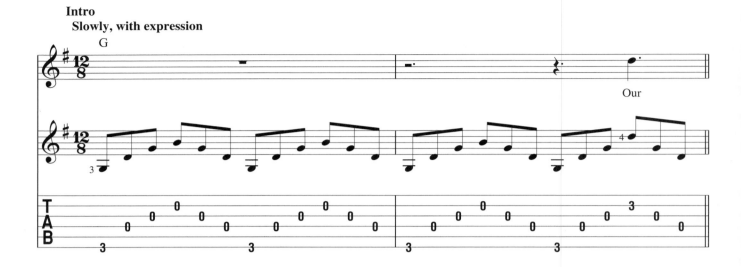

Verse

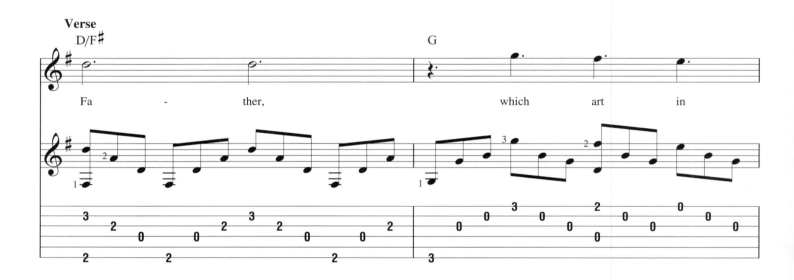

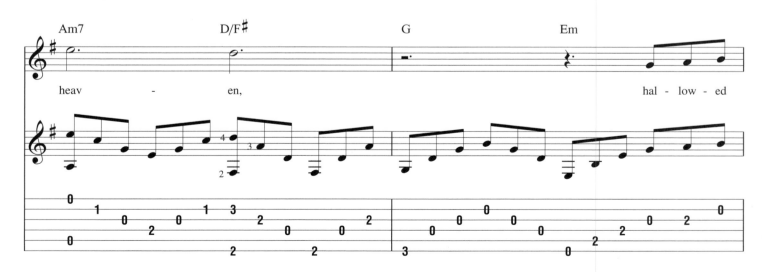

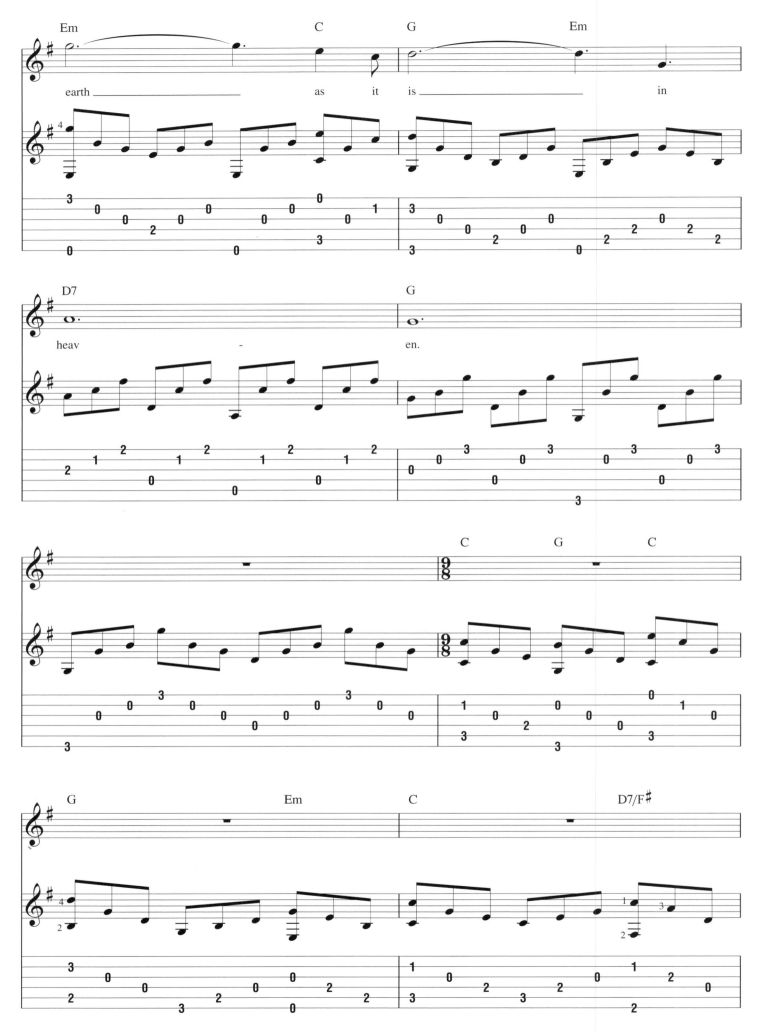

Love Me Tender

Words and Music by Elvis Presley and Vera Matson

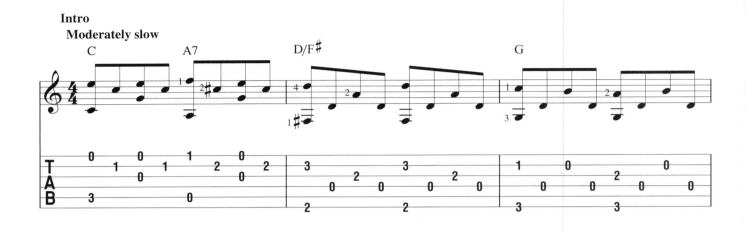

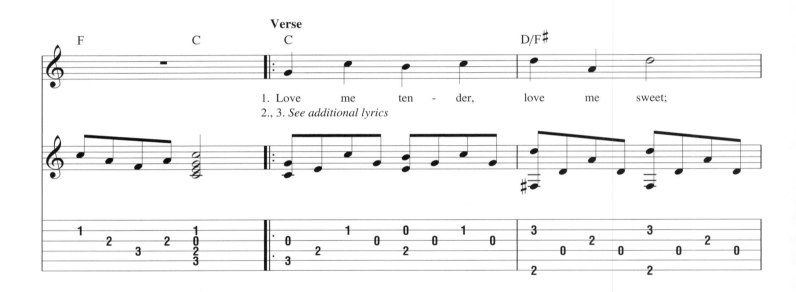

1. Love me ten - der, love me sweet;
2., 3. *See additional lyrics*

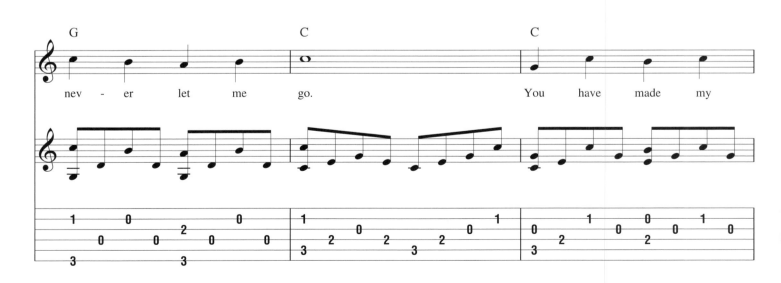

nev - er let me go. You have made my

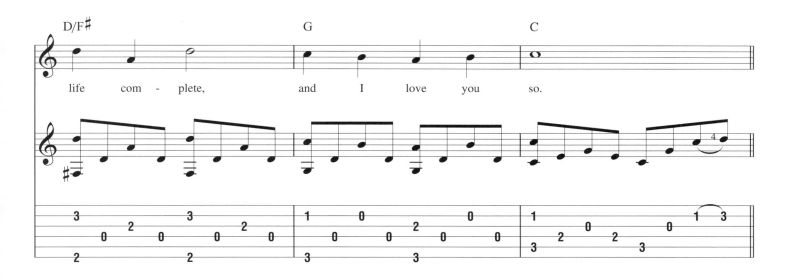

life com - plete, and I love you so.

Chorus

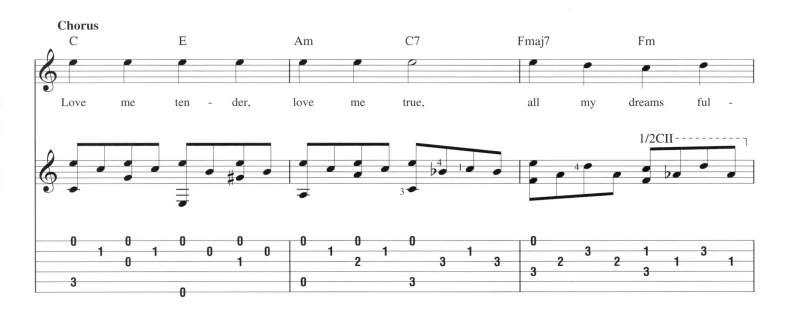

Love me ten - der, love me true, all my dreams ful -

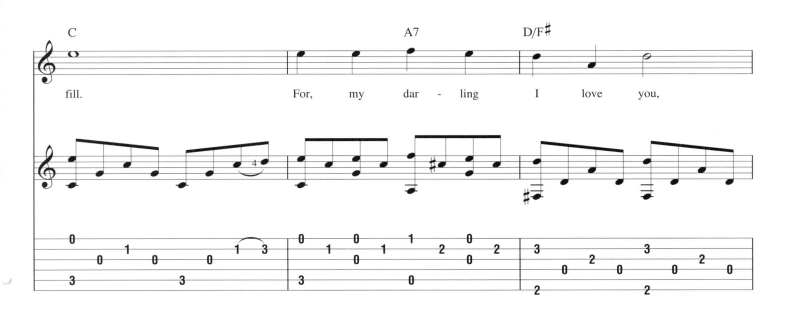

fill. For, my dar - ling I love you,

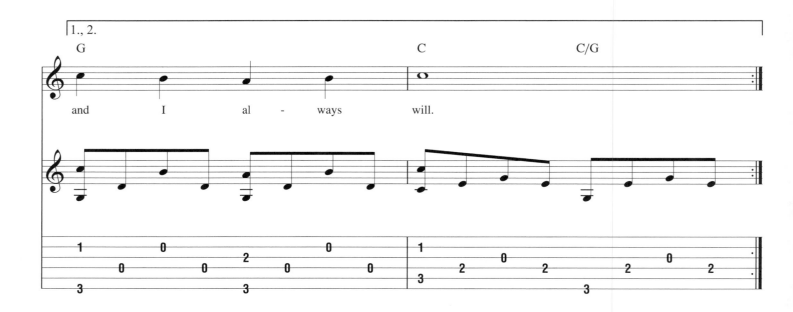

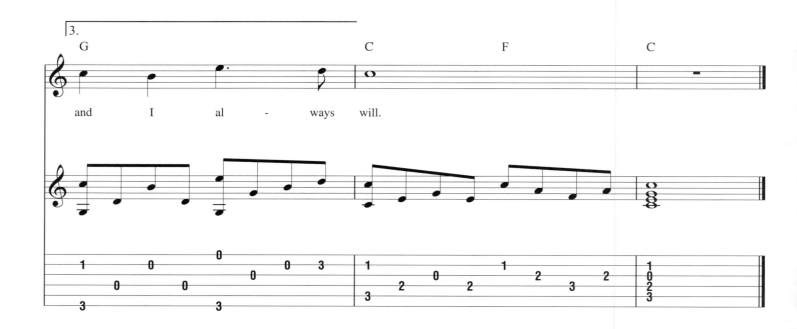

Additional Lyrics

2. Love me tender, love me long;
   Take me to your heart.
   For it's there that I belong,
   And we'll never part.

3. Love me tender, love me dear;
   Tell me you are mine.
   I'll be yours through all the years,
   Till the end of time.

This Is the Day

(A Wedding Song)

Words and Music by Scott Wesley Brown

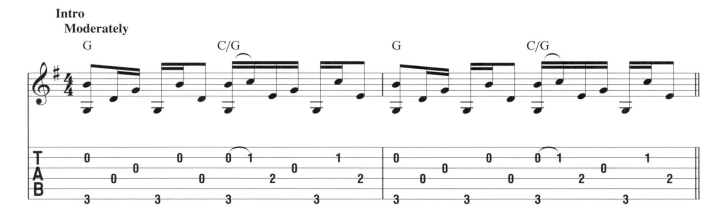

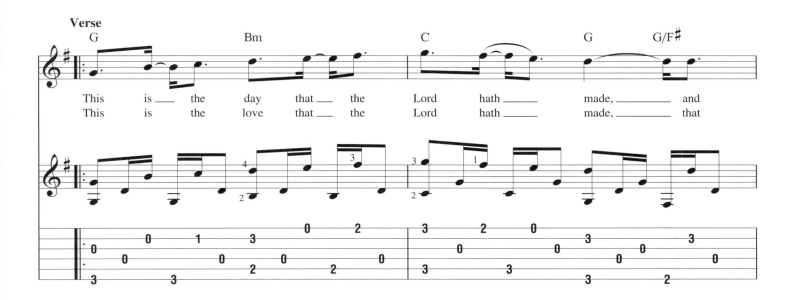

This is the day that the Lord hath made, and
This is the love that the Lord hath made, that

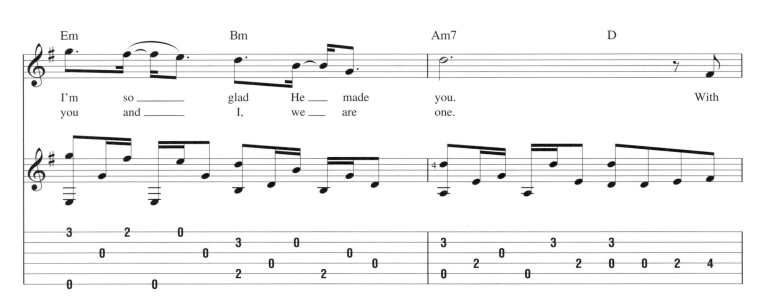

I'm so glad He made you.
you and I, we are one.

With

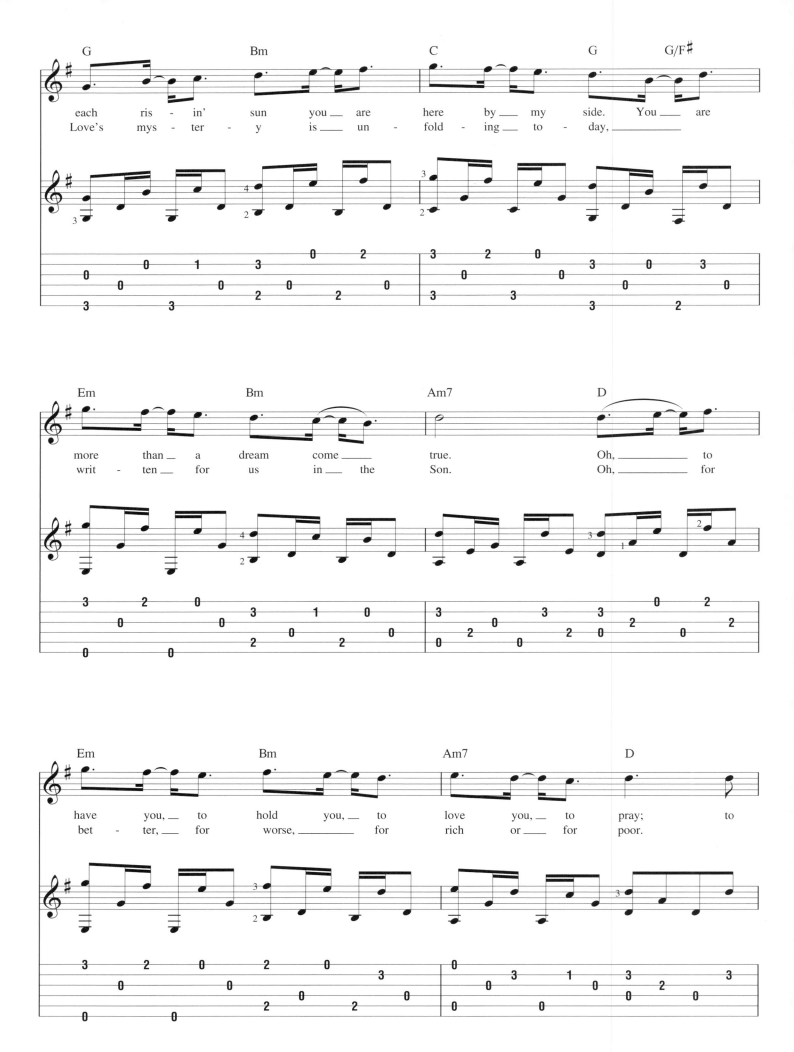

each   ris - in'   sun   you __ are   here   by __ my   side.   You __ are
Love's   mys - ter - y   is __ un - fold - ing __ to - day, _____

more   than __ a   dream   come _____   true.   Oh, _____ to
writ - ten __ for   us   in __ the   Son.   Oh, _____ for

have   you, __ to   hold   you, __ to   love   you, __ to   pray;   to
bet - ter, __ for   worse, _____ for   rich   or __ for   poor.

share with, __ to care with, __ to hold hands __ and say: _____
Each day __ that pass - es _____ I'll love __ you more, _____ 'cause

Chorus

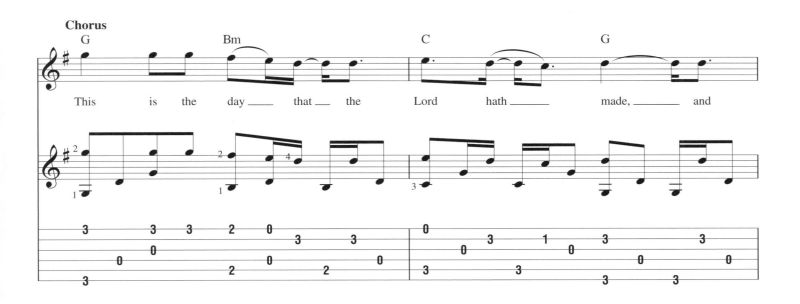

This is the day __ that __ the Lord hath _____ made, _____ and

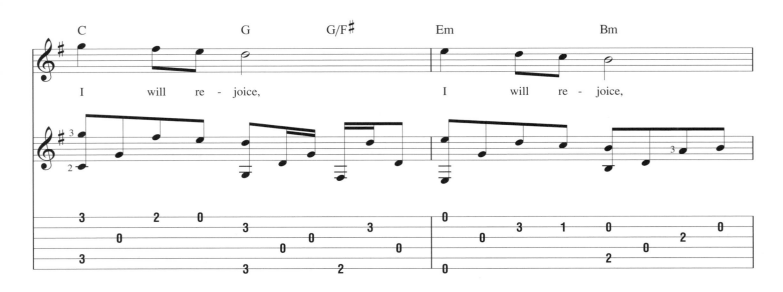

I will re - joice, I will re - joice,

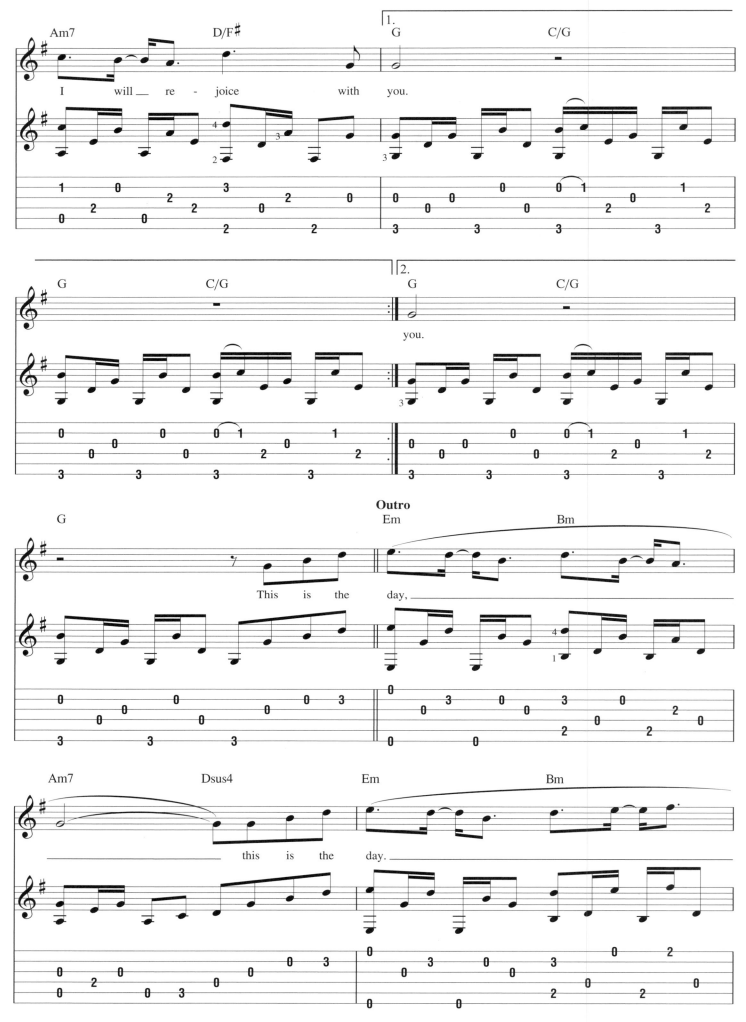

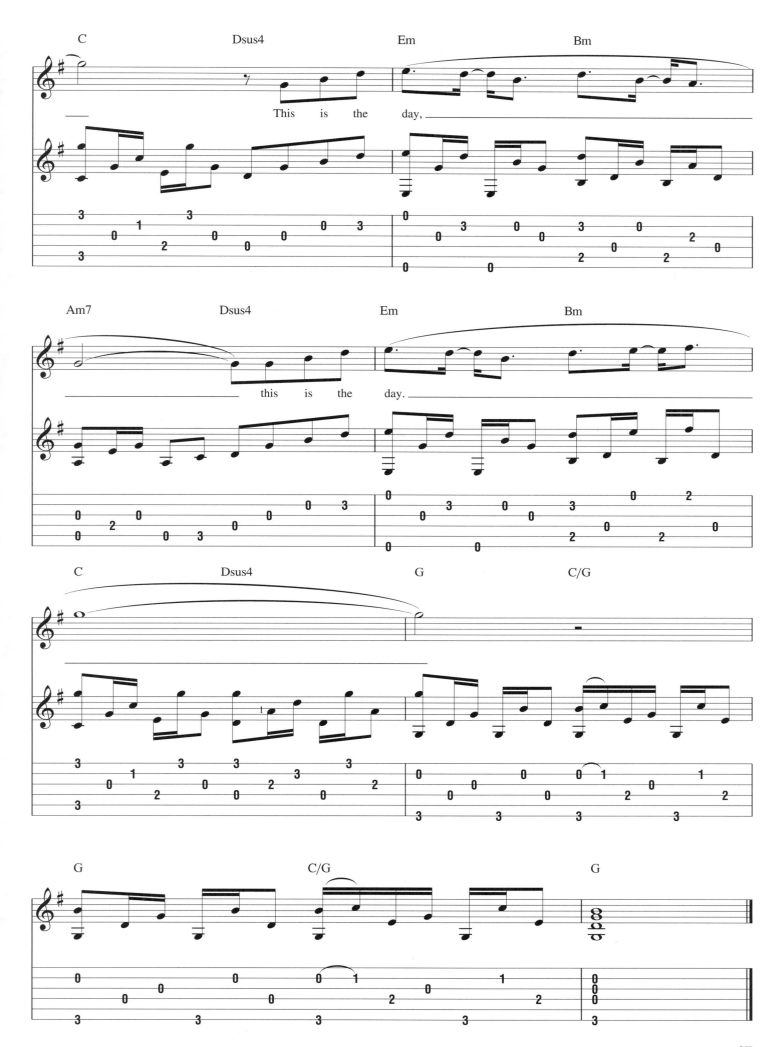

Wedding Processional

from THE SOUND OF MUSIC

Lyrics by Oscar Hammerstein II
Music by Richard Rodgers

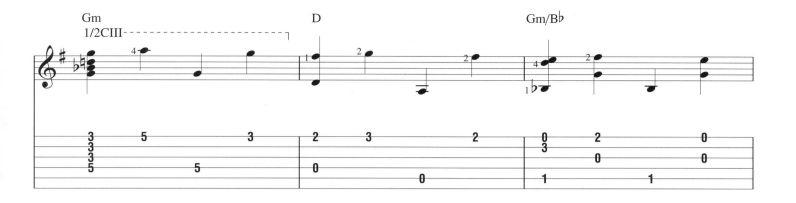

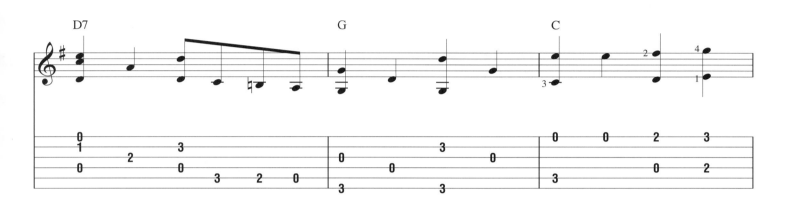

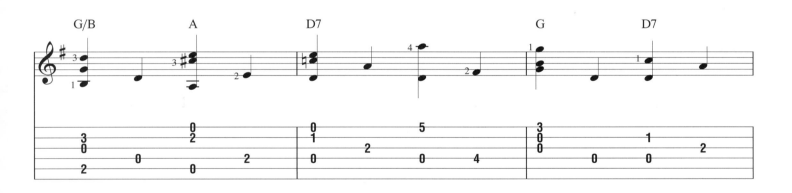

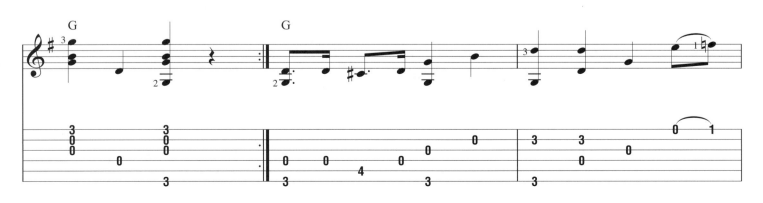

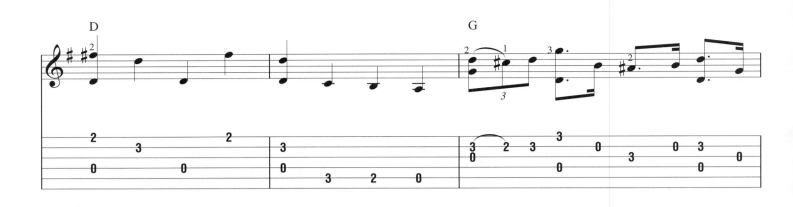

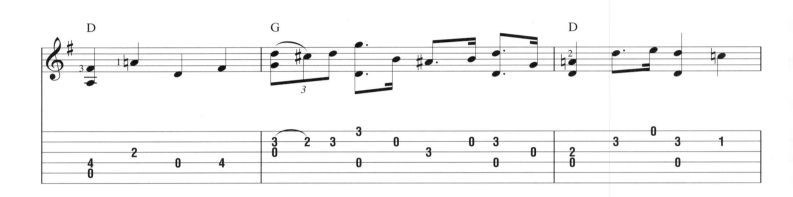

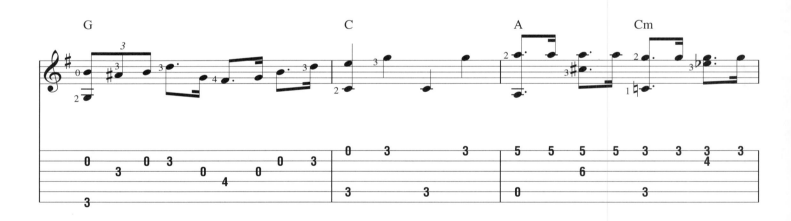

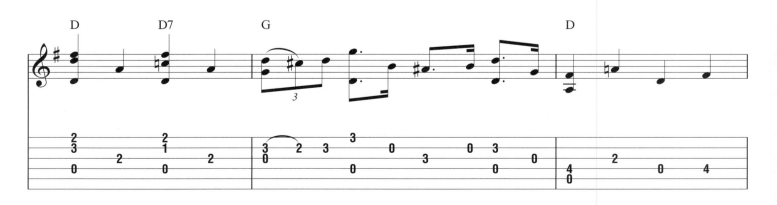

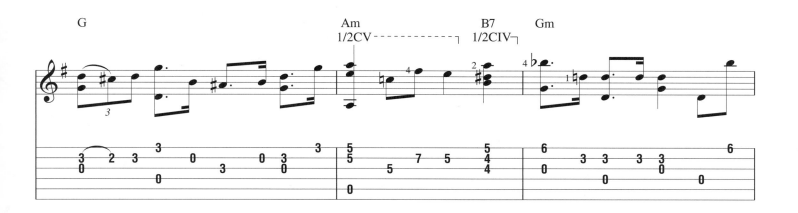

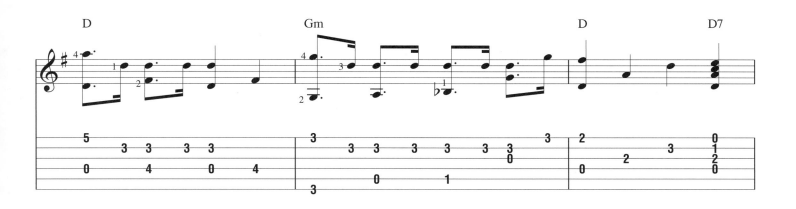

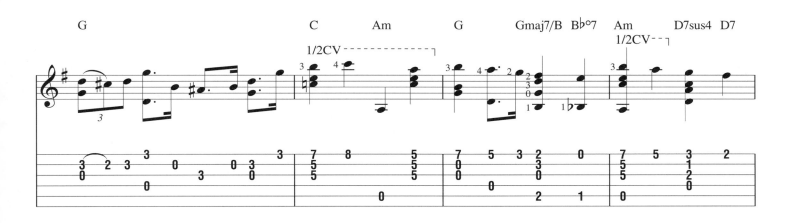

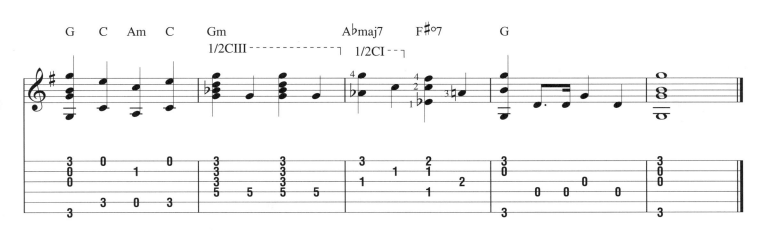

When You Say Nothing At All

Words and Music by Don Schlitz and Paul Overstreet

Tuning:
(low to high) D-A-D-G-B-E

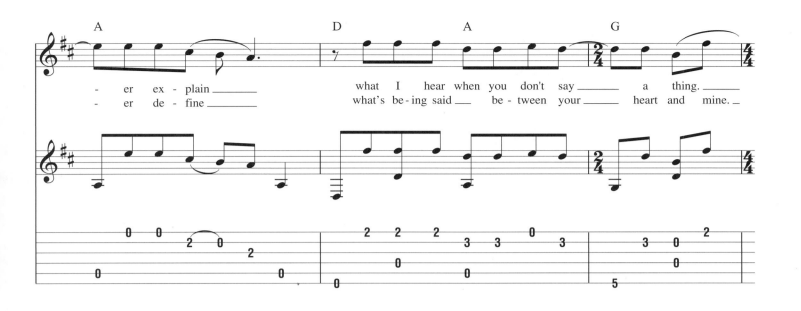

-er ex - plain _____ what I hear when you don't say _____ a thing. _____
-er de - fine _____ what's be - ing said _____ be - tween your _____ heart and mine. _

𝄋 **Chorus**

The smile on your face _ lets me know _ that you need _ me. There's a

truth in your eyes _ say - ing you'll _ nev - er leave _ me. A touch of your _ hand says you'll _

catch me if ____ ev - er I fall.   Now

To Coda ⊕ | 1.

Interlude

you say it best ___   when you say noth - ing at all. _____

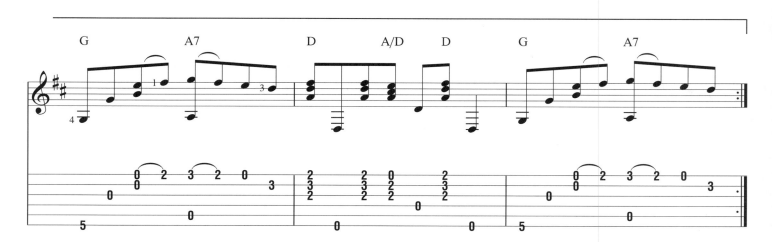

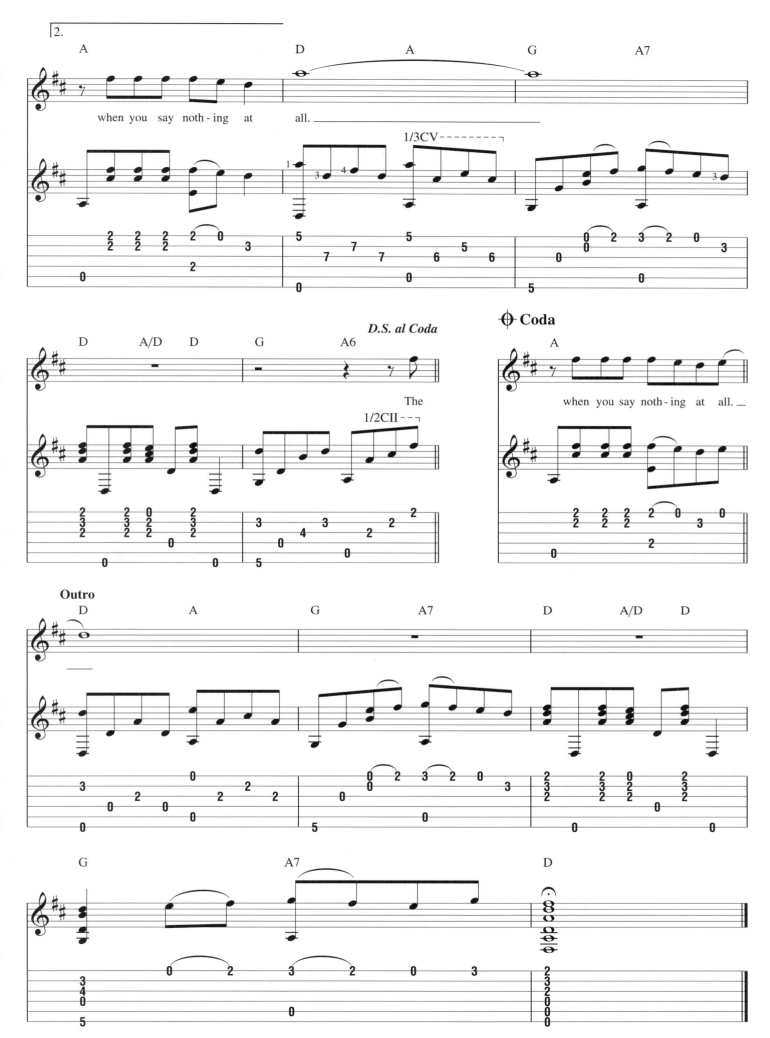

We've Only Just Begun

Words and Music by Roger Nichols and Paul Williams

56

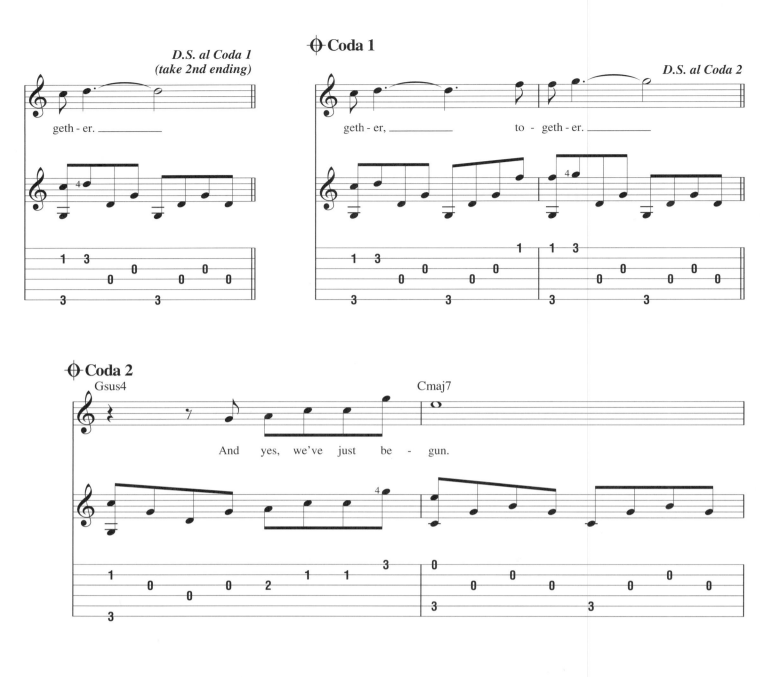

Additional Lyrics

2. Before the rising sun we fly,
   So many roads to choose,
   We start out walking and learn to run.
   And yes, we've just begun.

3., 4. And when the evening comes we smile,
   So much of life ahead,
   We'll find a place where there's room to grow.
   And yes, we've just begun.

You and I

Words and Music by Stevie Wonder

Drop D tuning:
(low to high) D-A-D-G-B-E

Verse
Slowly

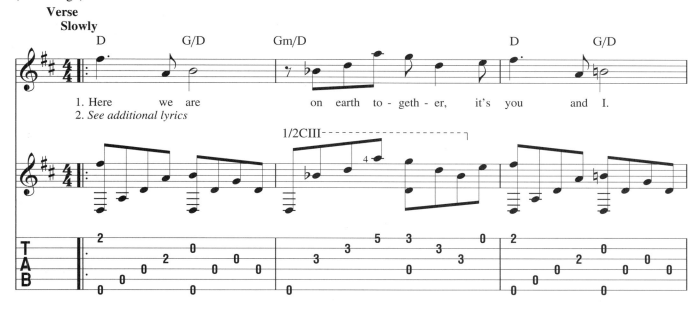

1. Here we are on earth to-geth-er, it's you and I.
2. *See additional lyrics*

God ___ has made ___ us fall in ___ love, it's true. ___ I've

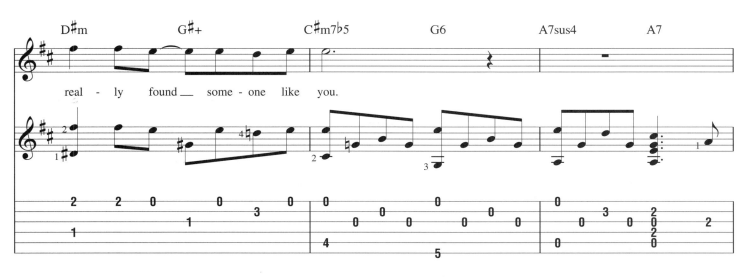

real-ly found ___ some-one like you.

Additional Lyrics

2. I am glad, at least in my life, I found someone
That may not be here forever to see me through.
But I found strength in you.
I only pray that I have shown you a brighter day,
Because that's all that I am living for, you see.
Don't worry what happens to me.
'Cause in my mind you will stay here always.
In love, you and I. You and I. You and I.

FINGERPICKING
GUITAR BOOKS

Hone your fingerpicking skills with these great songbooks featuring solo guitar arrangements in standard notation and tablature. The arrangements in these books are carefully written for intermediate-level guitarists. Each song combines melody and harmony in one superb guitar fingerpicking arrangement. Each book also includes an introduction to basic fingerstyle guitar.

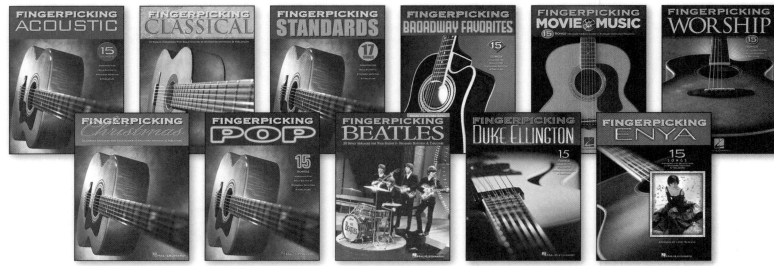

FINGERPICKING ACOUSTIC
00699614...$10.99

FINGERPICKING ACOUSTIC ROCK
00699764...$9.99

FINGERPICKING BACH
00699793...$8.95

FINGERPICKING BALLADS
00699717...$9.99

FINGERPICKING BEATLES
00699049...$19.99

FINGERPICKING BROADWAY FAVORITES
00699843...$9.99

FINGERPICKING BROADWAY HITS
00699838...$7.99

FINGERPICKING CELTIC FOLK
00701148...$7.99

FINGERPICKING CHILDREN'S SONGS
00699712...$9.99

FINGERPICKING CHRISTMAS
00699599...$8.95

FINGERPICKING CHRISTMAS CLASSICS
00701695...$7.99

FINGERPICKING CLASSICAL
00699620...$8.95

FINGERPICKING COUNTRY
00699687...$9.99

FINGERPICKING DISNEY
00699711...$9.95

FINGERPICKING DUKE ELLINGTON
00699845...$9.99

FINGERPICKING ENYA
00701161...$9.99

FINGERPICKING HYMNS
00699688...$8.95

FINGERPICKING ANDREW LLOYD WEBBER
00699839...$9.99

FINGERPICKING MOVIE MUSIC
00699919...$9.99

FINGERPICKING MOZART
00699794...$8.95

FINGERPICKING POP
00699615...$9.99

FINGERPICKING PRAISE
00699714...$8.95

FINGERPICKING ROCK
00699716...$9.99

FINGERPICKING STANDARDS
00699613...$9.99

FINGERPICKING WEDDING
00699637...$9.99

FINGERPICKING WORSHIP
00700554...$7.99

FINGERPICKING YULETIDE
00699654...$9.99

FOR MORE INFORMATION, SEE YOUR LOCAL MUSIC DEALER,
OR WRITE TO:

HAL•LEONARD®
CORPORATION
7777 W. BLUEMOUND RD. P.O. BOX 13819 MILWAUKEE, WI 53213

Visit Hal Leonard online at **www.halleonard.com**

Prices, contents and availability subject to change without notice.

0910

INCLUDES FULL PERFORMANCE CD

The **Wedding Essentials** series is a great resource for wedding musicians, featuring beautiful arrangements for a variety of instruments. Each book includes a reference CD to help couples choose the perfect songs for their wedding ceremony or reception. The CD is playable on any CD player, and is also enhanced so Mac and PC users can adjust the recording to any tempo without changing the pitch!

Christian Wedding Favorites

Answered Prayer • God Causes All Things to Grow • God Knew That I Needed You • Household of Faith • I Will Be Here • If You Could See What I See • Love Will Be Our Home • Seekers of Your Heart • This Day • 'Til the End of Time.

00311941 P/V/G.. $16.99

Contemporary Wedding Ballads

Beautiful in My Eyes • Bless the Broken Road • Endless Love • (Everything I Do) I Do It for You • From This Moment On • Have I Told You Lately • Here and Now • Love of a Lifetime • More Than Words • When You Say You Love Me.

00311942 P/V/G.. $16.99

Love Songs for Weddings

Grow Old with Me • Here, There and Everywhere • If • Longer • Part of My Heart • Valentine • We've Only Just Begun • The Wedding Song • You and I • You Raise Me Up.

00311943 Piano Solo.. $16.99

Service Music for Weddings

Processionals, Recessionals, Lighting of the Unity Candle

Allegro maestoso • Amazing Grace • Ave Maria • Canon in D • Jesu, Joy of Man's Desiring • Jupiter (Chorale Theme) • O Perfect Love • Ode to Joy • Rondeau • Trumpet Voluntary.

00311944 Piano Solo.. $14.99

Wedding Guitar Solos

All I Ask of You • Gabriel's Oboe • Grow Old with Me • Hallelujah • Here, There and Everywhere • More Than Words • Sunrise, Sunset • Wedding Song (There Is Love) • When I Fall in Love • You Raise Me Up.

00701335 Guitar Solo.. $16.99

Wedding Vocal Solos

Grow Old with Me • I Swear • In My Life • Longer • The Promise (I'll Never Say Goodbye) • Someone Like You • Sunrise, Sunset • Till There Was You • Time After Time • We've Only Just Begun.

00311945 High Voice... $16.99
00311946 Low Voice.. $16.99

Worship for Weddings

Be Unto Your Name • Broken and Beautiful • Center • He Is Here • Here and Now • Holy Ground • How Beautiful • Listen to Our Hearts • Today (As for Me and My House).

00311949 P/V/G.. $16.99

FOR MORE INFORMATION, SEE YOUR LOCAL MUSIC DEALER, OR WRITE TO:

HAL•LEONARD® CORPORATION

7777 W. BLUEMOUND RD. P.O. BOX 13819 MILWAUKEE, WI 53213

www.halleonard.com

Prices, content, and availability subject to change without notice.

0810

Must-Have Collections for Every Guitarist!

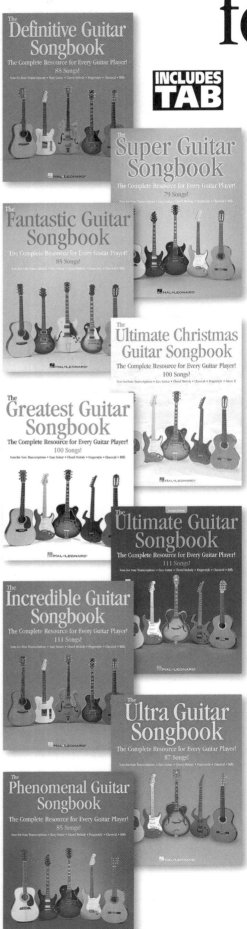

INCLUDES TAB

The Definitive Guitar Songbook

There's something for every guitarist in this amazing collection! It features 88 songs in all styles of music and all forms of notation, including: Guitar Recorded Versions (Birthday • Ramblin' Man); Easy Guitar with Notes & Tab (Blackbird • Don't Be Cruel); Easy Guitar (Baby Love • Cheek to Cheek • Young Americans); Chord Melody Guitar (I Could Write a Book • When I Fall in Love); Classical Guitar (Gavotte • Prelude); Fingerstyle Guitar (Imagine • My One and Only Love); and Guitar Riffs (Fire and Rain • Maggie May • Twist and Shout).
00699267 Guitar Collection $19.95

The Fantastic Guitar Songbook

85 tunes in a wide variety of notation formats (easy guitar with and without tablature, chord melody guitar, classical, fingerstyle, riffs and note-for-note tab transcriptions), and in a range of musical styles – from pop/rock hits to jazz standards, movie songs to Motown, country, classical and everything in between. Includes: ABC • Canon in D • Drops of Jupiter • Hey Jude • I Am a Man of Constant Sorrow • Jack and Diane • Leader of the Band • Mama, I'm Coming Home • Summer of '69 • So Nice (Summer Samba) • Tush • We've Only Just Begun • Yellow Submarine • and more.
00699561 Guitar Collection $19.95

The Greatest Guitar Songbook

This comprehensive collection for all guitarists includes 100 songs in genres from jazz standards, to pop/rock favorites, Motown masterpieces and movie music, to traditional tunes, country numbers and classical pieces. Notation styles include: note-for-note transcriptions (Sweet Child O' Mine • Wild Thing); Easy Guitar with Notes & Tab (Day Tripper • Für Elise • Misty); Easy Guitar (Boot Scootin' Boogie • Unchained Melody); Fingerstyle Guitar (Amazing Grace • Greensleeves); and Guitar Riffs (Angie • Layla • My Girl); and more!
00699142 Guitar Collection $20.95

The Incredible Guitar Songbook

Features a whopping 111 songs in genres from blues to jazz to pop and rock to classical and country, and a variety of notation styles, including: Note-for-note transcriptions in notes and tab (Tears in Heaven • Wonderwall); Easy Guitar with Notes and Tab (All Shook Up • Bésame Mucho • Pride and Joy); Easy Guitar, No Tab (Michelle • Route 66); Chord Melody Guitar (Satin Doll); Classical Guitar (Bourée • Pavane); Fingerstyle Guitar (Something); and Guitar Riffs (Beast of Burden • Gloria).
00699245 Guitar Collection $19.95

The Phenomenal Guitar Songbook

This remarkable book features 85 songs from all styles of music. It includes a variety of note-for-note transcriptions, riffs, and arrangements for easy guitar, chord melody, fingerstyle, and classical guitar. Songs include: Ain't Too Proud to Beg • Blue Skies • California Dreamin' • Fly like an Eagle • Fur Elise • Giant Steps • God Bless the U.S.A. • Good Vibrations • Green Onions • In My Life • Moon River • My Way • Proud Mary • Redneck Woman • Under the Bridge • What's Going On • You Are My Sunshine • and more!
00699759 Guitar Collection $19.99

The Super Guitar Songbook

The latest songbook in our wildly popular series of mixed collections of guitar arrangements and transcriptions. This book features 79 songs in a wide variety of music styles and notation formats: Guitar Recorded Versions, fingerstyle, easy guitar with notes and tab, classical, chord melody, and riffs! These books truly grow with the player! Songs include: Bewitched • California Girls • Come to My Window • (Everything I Do) I Do It for You • In a Sentimental Mood • Lucy in the Sky with Diamonds • Oye Como Va • Rocky Top • Scuttle Buttin' • Sharp Dressed Man • Soul Man • You'll Be in My Heart • and more!
00699618 Guitar Collection $19.99

The Ultimate Christmas Guitar Songbook

100 songs in a variety of notation styles, from easy guitar and classical guitar arrangements to note-for-note guitar tab transcriptions. Includes: All Through the Night • Auld Lang Syne • Blue Christmas • The Chipmunk Song • The Gift • (There's No Place Like) Home for the Holidays • I've Got My Love to Keep Me Warm • Jingle Bells • My Favorite Things • One Bright Star • Rockin' Around the Christmas Tree • Santa Baby • Silver Bells • Wonderful Christmastime • and more.
00700185 Guitar Collection $19.95

The Ultimate Guitar Songbook – Second Edition

110 songs in all genres and guitar styles: everything from pop/rock hits to jazz standards, Motown masterpieces to movie classics, traditional tunes, country favorites, Broadway blockbusters and beyond! Features note-for-note transcriptions, riffs, and arrangements for easy guitar, chord melody, fingerstyle, classical & more!
00699909 Guitar Collection $19.99

The Ultra Guitar Songbook

The latest edition in our popular series featuring multiple notation styles, perfect for players looking for a little variety in their playing! This collection features 87 songs in Guitar Recorded Versions notation (Bad Moon Rising • Hot for Teacher); Easy Guitar (Bennie and the Jets • Free Fallin' • Ring of Fire • Tainted Love); Chord Melody Guitar (Come Fly with Me • Witchcraft); Classical Guitar (Capricho Arabe • Minuet in G); Fingerstyle Guitar (Every Rose Has Its Thorn • Fields of Gold); Guitar Riffs (Beautiful Girls • Dancing with Myself); and many more!
00700130 Guitar Collection $19.95

Prices, contents, and availability subject to change without notice.

FOR MORE INFORMATION, SEE YOUR LOCAL MUSIC DEALER, OR WRITE TO:

HAL•LEONARD® CORPORATION
7777 W. BLUEMOUND RD. P.O. BOX 13819 MILWAUKEE, WI 53213

www.halleonard.com

0210